BARBADOS TRAVEL GUIDE 2024

Comprehensive Guide to Barbados Best-Kept
Secrets With Maps, Pictures, Best Cuisines,
Accomodation, Navigating History, Culture of
the Caribbean Island

By

Libby Martinez

Table of Contents

INTRODUCTION

Barbados: My enchanting journey

Everything started with the thrill of leaving my busy hometown behind. As soon as I stepped into the aircraft, I could feel the excitement of adventure rushing through me. The airport was bustling with expectation. As I took my seat, I looked forward to the hours that were ahead of me, knowing that every second would bring me one step closer to the Caribbean paradise that lay ahead of me.

I saw Barbados for the first time as the jet landed; it was an amazing mosaic of clear beaches, emerald oceans, and lush flora. The balmy wind embraced me like an old friend as soon as I stepped onto the tarmac, quickly wiping away any last remnants of travel weary.

My lodging, which was tucked away along the shore, was a tranquil haven where I could relax and take in everything that the island has to offer. The real experience started from that point on.

Discovering the energetic capital, Bridgetown, was a really engaging experience. The vibrant markets, kind residents, and colorful buildings all greeted me warmly. I became fully engrossed in the pace of Barbados life, relishing each minute as I meandered around the streets, trying out regional cuisine, and taking in the rich cultural offerings of the island.

Naturally, a visit to Barbados would not be complete without taking advantage of its famed beaches for some sunbathing. Every strip of beach gave a little piece of heaven, from the pristine coastlines of Crane Beach to the secluded coves of Bottom Bay. A kaleidoscope of marine life, including colorful coral reefs and playful sea turtles moving elegantly under the surface, was visible to snorkelers in the glistening clean seas.

I traveled inland and found a verdant interior full with natural treasures. Barbados' varied beauty amazed me when I hiked through the lush Welchman Hall Gully and explored the mysterious Harrison's Cave.

The enticing smells of Bajan food wafted from small cafes throughout the evenings. Every meal, including the island's famous rum drinks, was a culinary marvel, from the fiery jerk chicken to the delicious flying fish.

The people' friendliness, kindness, and contagious enthusiasm for life, however, may have been the most memorable experiences for me. They left a lasting impression on my heart. I felt completely welcomed by the spirit of Barbados, whether I was dancing to the throbbing beats of calypso music or just sitting under the stars telling tales.

As my trip was coming to a conclusion, I discovered that I was hesitant to leave this magical island paradise. But in addition to memories, I also brought a strong feeling of thankfulness for the relationships and experiences I had while I was in Barbados with me as I boarded the aircraft to return home.

About Barbados

Greetings from Barbados, a treasure of the Caribbean known for its clear beaches, lively culture, and kind people. Barbados, tucked away in the eastern Caribbean Sea, entices tourists from all over the globe with an allure that combines breathtaking scenery and a rich cultural legacy.

1. Beaches: Barbados is home to some of the Caribbean's most beautiful beaches. Every length of coastline provides a little piece of heaven, from the serene turquoise seas of Carlisle Bay to the pristine white sands of Crane Beach. Amidst the stunning coastal backdrop, guests may enjoy swimming, snorkeling, sunbathing, and water sports.

2. Culture and Heritage: Take in the intricate cultural fabric of Barbados, which has been molded by centuries of history and customs. Discover the island's colonial heritage at St. Nicholas Abbey, explore the UNESCO-listed Bridgetown and its ancient Garrison, or stroll through Holetown's colorful streets during the annual Crop Over Festival, which is a spectacular celebration of Bajan song, dancing, and culture.

3. gastronomic Delights: Get ready for an unparalleled gastronomic experience. Barbados is a culinary enthusiast's dream come true, with a mouthwatering variety of tastes inspired by British, Caribbean, and African cuisines. Indulge in rum tasting at one of the island's distilleries, enjoy freshly caught seafood at seaside eateries, and sample local specialties like pepperpot stew, cou-cou, and flying fish.

4. Adventure & Recreation: Barbados offers plenty of opportunities for thrill-seekers. Hike through the verdant interior to discover secret waterfalls and picturesque paths, surf the world-class waves at Soup Bowl or Bathsheba, or dive into the depths of Carlisle Bay to uncover shipwrecks alive with marine life.

5. Luxurious Resorts & Lodging: Barbados has a variety of lodging options to fit every preference and price range, whether you're looking for an opulent beachside getaway or a little boutique hotel tucked away in the countryside. You may enjoy comfort and elegance in the middle of stunning settings at everything from modest guesthouses to all-inclusive resorts.

6. Warm Hospitality: The friendliness and kindness of Barbados' people is one of the best things about traveling there. The people from the island, called Bajans, are very friendly and willing to share their customs, culture, and island secrets with guests.

7. Barbados is a popular holiday destination for people of all ages and interests because of its reputation for safety and accessibility. The island's English-speaking populace, modern infrastructure, and effective transit system guarantee a seamless and pleasurable stay for tourists from all over the world.

In summary, Barbados enthralls visitors with its unspoiled beauty, vibrant culture, and kind demeanor. Whether you're looking for outdoor adventure, beach relaxation, or a chance to immerse yourself in the native way of life, Barbados has something to offer everyone. You will want to come back time and time again.

Discover the Unique Culture of Barbados

1. Barbados's most famous celebration, the Crop Over Festival, marks the conclusion of the sugar cane harvest

and is the climax of the island's cultural calendar. Usually, it starts in June and ends with the Grand Kadooment Day procession in early August. Bright parades, energetic street gatherings, calypso contests, and traditional Bajan food are all part of the festivities. Since its beginnings in the 17th century, the festival has grown to become one of the most eagerly awaited occasions in the Caribbean.

2. Holetown Festival: This yearly celebration honors the 1627 arrival of the first English immigrants in Barbados and takes place at Holetown, St. James Parish. Typically held in February, the week-long event includes street fairs, live music, historical reenactments, artisan markets, and a vibrant procession. Indulge in the vibrant ambiance of this ancient town while getting a taste of Bajan culture.

3. Oistins Fish Festival: This Easter weekend celebration honors Barbados' culinary and nautical traditions and takes place in the fishing community of Oistins. Visitors may savor a variety of freshly cooked seafood delights, such as flying fish, dolphin, and lobster. Foodies and culture lovers should not miss the event, which also includes boat races, fishing contests, live music, and cultural shows.

4. Holders Season: World-class performances in music, theater, dance, and literature are part of a series of cultural activities hosted at Holders House, a historic plantation home in St. James Parish. Renowned singers

and artists from all over the world come to town during the season, which usually spans from February to April. Holders House offers a sophisticated setting for literary readings, theater shows, and outdoor concerts.

5. Barbados Food and Rum Festival: This gourmet spectacle honors both the island nation's role as the rum's origin and its rich culinary legacy. A series of tastings, cooking demos, and gourmet events highlight the island's best chefs, mixologists, and culinary artists. The festival takes place in October. A variety of Bajan foods, rum drinks, and handcrafted goods are available for visitors to try as they take in live entertainment and music.

6. Reggae Festival: Every year in April, Barbados celebrates its love affair with reggae music with an annual Reggae Festival. The event includes dancehall, soca, and calypso performers in addition to performances by regional and worldwide reggae musicians. Throughout the island, there are several locations hosting concerts, beach parties, and jam sessions where guests can groove to the catchy rhythms of reggae music.

7. Barbados Independence Day is observed on November 30th in honor of the island nation's 1966 declaration of independence from British colonial authority. There are parades, flag-raising ceremonies, cultural events, and fireworks displays to celebrate the nation's passion for patriotism. Guests are welcome to

participate in the celebrations and feel the pride and happiness of the Bajan people as they mark this important historical achievement.

These are just a few of the many colorful festivals and events that Barbados hosts all year long. Whatever your interests—music, cuisine, or history—there's always something intriguing going on on this charming island.

Barbados' Time Zone

Throughout the year, Barbados follows Atlantic Standard Time (AST). Barbados, however, adopts Atlantic Daylight Time (ADT) during daylight saving time, which normally begins on the second Sunday in March and ends on the first Sunday in November.

Below is a breakdown of Barbados' time zone:

Atlantic Standard Time (AST) is the standard time.
- Coordinated Universal Time (UTC-4) is 4 hours behind AST.

Atlantic Daylight Time (ADT) is used for Daylight Saving Time.
Barbados shifts one hour ahead of UTC during daylight saving time.

Because of its closeness to the equator, Barbados has no notable variations in daylight hours throughout the year. As a result, the main purpose of the switch to daylight saving time is to synchronize the island's time with other places that do follow it, such certain areas of North America and Europe.

It is imperative that tourists remain cognizant of Barbados' time zone, particularly in the event of making travel or activity plans.

Things to Think About Before Leaving

1. Verify Barbados' entrance criteria, particularly those on passport validity and visa needs. Certain foreign visitors may need a visa, while others may be able to enter the country without one or get one upon arrival. Make sure the duration of your passport is at least six months longer than the desired stay.

2. Health Cautions: Speak with your doctor about any shots or preventative measures that may be necessary before visiting Barbados. Think about getting evacuation and medical emergency coverage while traveling, along with COVID-19 coverage if necessary.

3. Weather & environment: Barbados has year-round mild temperatures due to its tropical environment. But it's vital to remember that hurricane season, which normally lasts from June to November, occurs. Keep an eye on weather reports and think about purchasing travel insurance that covers interruptions caused by inclement weather.

4. Money and Banking: The Barbados dollar (BBD) is the unit of money used there. Even though US dollars are accepted everywhere, it's a good idea to have some local money on hand for minor purchases and transactions. Major cities and popular tourist destinations have ATMs; nevertheless, to prevent any problems while using your debit or credit cards overseas, let your bank know about your trip schedule.

5. Transportation: Arrange your means of getting about Barbados. You may utilize a taxi, a rental vehicle, a public bus, or a private transfer. The left side of the road is used for driving, and overall, the state of the roads are favorable. For navigation, think about getting a local map or renting a GPS.

6. Accommodations: Do your homework and reserve your lodging well in advance, particularly during the busiest travel times of the year, like the winter. There are many different places to stay in Barbados, such as guesthouses, boutique hotels, luxury resorts, and vacation rentals. Select lodging options based on your spending limit and preferences.

7. Barbados is a relatively secure place for people to visit, but you should still use common sense and take safety steps to make sure you're safe. Steer clear of nighttime solo strolls in strange places, lock up your belongings, and keep an eye out for small-time robbery. Keep up with local news and travel advisories, and follow any government-issued warnings.

8. Cultural manners: To guarantee polite encounters with the locals, familiarize yourself with Barbados' traditions and manners. Because Bajans are recognized for their warmth and hospitality, remember to be courteous, smile when you meet someone, and conduct yourself in conversation with decency and decency.

9. Activities and Attractions: Whether you want to explore ancient places, unwind on immaculate beaches, or indulge in Bajan cuisine, research the activities and attractions you'd want to enjoy in Barbados. To guarantee your space, think about scheduling tours or excursions in advance, particularly for well-liked activities like catamaran cruises, diving, and snorkeling.

10. COVID-19 guidelines: Keep yourself updated on Barbados travel restrictions and the most recent COVID-19 guidelines. This could include immunization, testing, and quarantine guidelines. Before you go, get the most recent information by visiting the official government website or getting in touch with your airline.

You can make sure your trip to Barbados is trouble-free and pleasurable by taking these things into account before you go. Barbados is a stunning Caribbean island.

Barbados's Transportation Options

1. Hiring a Vehicle:
- Among the easiest ways to see Barbados is by renting a vehicle.

Both domestic and foreign rental agencies are present on the island, along with many international ones.

- Similar to the UK, driving is done on the left side of the road, and traffic signs are posted in English.

- Drivers must be at least 21 years old and have a valid driver's license from their native country.

For navigation, think about getting a local map or renting a GPS, particularly if you want to go off the usual route.

2. Buses for the Public:

- The Barbados Transport Board (blue buses) and privately owned yellow buses run an extensive public bus network in Barbados.

- The bus system is an inexpensive and widely accessible mode of transportation across the majority of the island.

- Bus timetables may be less frequent in rural locations, although they operate often along important routes.

Upon boarding, passengers pay the driver in cash for their fare; precise change is advised.

- Bus stations are easily identifiable, and each bus has a display on the front with route information.

3. Taxis:

- Taxis are easily found in Barbados and may be booked ahead of time or called on the street.

- Metered taxis are designated as official taxis by a "Z" on the license plate.

Before beginning the trip, it's a good idea to double check the fee with the driver since not all taxis have meters.

- Major tourist destinations, lodging facilities, and the airport all have taxi stands.
- When traveling short distances or visiting places that are difficult to get by public transit, taxis are a practical choice.

4. ZR Vans:

ZR vans are privately run minibuses that are well-liked by both residents and visitors as a means of transportation.
- These vans usually travel predetermined routes throughout the island and are identified by a yellow license plate.
- ZR vans may be seen parked on the side of the road, and passengers pay the driver immediately as they board.
- ZR vans are an affordable and practical kind of transportation, but they may not follow set timetables and become congested at rush hour.

5. Personal Transports:

- If you're looking for a more individualized and practical mode of transportation, think about scheduling private transfers or hiring a driver for the day.
- Private transport services are provided by several hotels and tour companies and may be scheduled in advance.
- Private transfers are great for comfortable and flexible sightseeing, day trips, and airport transfers.

It's advisable to enquire about costs in advance since private transport prices vary based on the journey's length and distance.

6. Cycling and strolling:
- Cycling or walking about Barbados is a wonderful way to see the island's natural beauty and culture.
- There are many of walkways and walking routes in popular tourist locations and along beaches.
- You may hire cruisers and mountain bikes from a number of businesses on the island to go around at your own speed.
- When walking or riding, be in mind that sidewalks and roadside areas may not have enough shade, so be sure to wear sunscreen, a hat, and comfortable shoes.

Barbados has a wide range of transportation choices to accommodate every taste and budget, making navigation comparatively simple. Discovering this beautiful Caribbean island is part of the experience, whether you decide to take a cab or private transport for convenience, take a public bus to interact with people, or rent a vehicle for independence and flexibility.

Barbados's Visas Requirements

Exemption from Visa:
Many nationalities' citizens may visit Barbados for tourism without a visa. These nations include the US, Canada, the UK, member states of the EU, Australia, New Zealand, and several more.

- Entry is often allowed to citizens of nations that do not need a visa for a certain amount of time, generally up to 90 days. The amount of time allowed to remain, however, may vary according on immigration discretion and nationality.

Visa upon arrival:
Certain nations who are not excluded from requiring a visa may be able to get one when they get to Barbados. With this option, visitors may apply for a visa as soon as they arrive at the point of entry, which might be an airport or seaport.
In order to secure a visa upon arrival, one may need to provide certain documents such as a valid passport, evidence of onward travel, proof of lodging, and enough cash to cover living costs.
To ensure you have the most recent information on eligibility and criteria for a visa, it is imperative that you verify with the Barbados Immigration Department or consulate/embassy.

Travel Authorization Electronically (ETA):
- For visitors from certain nations, Barbados has instituted the Electronic Travel Authorization (ETA) system. Before visiting Barbados, qualified travelers may apply online for entrance permission via the ETA.
- During the ETA application procedure, personal data, passport information, and information on the planned stay in Barbados are usually needed.

- After being authorized, the ETA permits entrance into Barbados for touristic reasons and is electronically connected to the traveler's passport.

Certain Countries' Requirements Regarding Visas:
- Specific visa requirements for visiting Barbados may vary from general visa procedures in certain countries. For comprehensive visa information, citizens of these nations should get in touch with the Barbados consulate or embassy that is closest to them.
Furthermore, visitors who have travel papers other than a passport or who are dual nationals should confirm the precise visa requirements that apply to them.

Extension of Visit:
- Before their allotted stay ends, travelers who want to remain longer than what is allowed must ask for an extension via the Barbados Immigration Department.
- Requests for extensions are considered individually, and acceptance is contingent upon compliance with immigration laws and regulations.

Before visiting Barbados, visitors should acquaint themselves with the country's visa requirements and make sure they are met. If you don't have the necessary documentation, you might be refused entry or face additional immigration repercussions. Furthermore, when visiting Barbados, visitors should always have the necessary paperwork with them, such as a current passport and any necessary visas or travel authorizations.

The Trip Cost to Barbados

When organizing a vacation to Barbados, a number of expenditures must be taken into account, such as lodging, transportation, food, activities, and other extras. The price of a tourist vacation to Barbados is broken down as follows:

1. Accommodation:

- There are many different ways to stay in Barbados, including guesthouses, vacation rentals, and exclusive resorts and boutique hotels.
- Costs vary based on the location, features, and season. You should budget at least $100 to $500 each night for lodging.
- For $50 to $100 a night, budget visitors can discover more economical choices, such as hostels or guesthouses.

2. Transport:
- Car rentals: The price of a car rental in Barbados varies based on the kind of car, length of the rental, and insurance coverage. Typically, daily fees fall between $50 and $150.
- Public buses: Depending on the distance traveled, public buses in Barbados offer rates ranging from $1 to $3 each journey, making them an inexpensive mode of transportation.
- Taxis: The cost of a taxi ride is metered; short-distance costs start at around $15 and go up depending on waiting time and length.
- ZR vans: Depending on the distance traveled, ZR van tickets range from $1 to $5, making them an affordable choice.

3. Dining and Food:
Barbados has a variety of dining establishments, from upmarket eateries to neighborhood street food sellers.

- A dinner at a high-end restaurant might cost up to $150 per person, but a meal at a mid-range restaurant usually costs between $15 and $50.
- For $5 to $15 a meal, tourists on a tight budget can dine at casual restaurants or street food vendors.

4. Events and Outings:
- The kind of experience and operator determine how much an activity or trip costs in Barbados.
- Popular pursuits like diving, snorkeling, catamaran excursions, and island tours may cost up to $200 per person.
- Admission costs for museums, historic institutions, and botanical gardens may vary from $5 to $20 per person.

5. Aside from the above:
- Other costs might include entertainment, shopping, tipping, and mementos.
- Set aside money for supplemental costs like sunscreen, bug repellent, water bottles, and beach gear.
Tipping is not required, although it is valued in Barbados. Tipping is customarily between 10% and 15% of the total cost at dining establishments and for services like tour guides and taxis.

6. Exchange rate and currency:
- The Barbados dollar (BBD) is the unit of currency used in Barbados. On the other hand, US dollars are often used, and prices are frequently given in both currencies.

- The US dollar and Barbadian dollar have a fixed exchange rate of around 2:1.

Total Spending:
- A vacation to Barbados will cost different amounts based on your travel style, length of stay, and personal preferences.
- A mid-range tourist's daily budget in Barbados may be as high as $300 or more, taking into account lodging, food, transportation, and activities.

To guarantee a delightful and unforgettable trip to Barbados, travelers must budget appropriately and make advance plans. To make the most of their vacation and successfully manage spending, tourists may research rates, compare choices, and establish a reasonable budget.

Top Hotels in Barbados for Lodging

Low Spending
1. Hotel Coconut Court Beach:
- Site: Christ Church, Hastings
- Price: $100 per night and above
- Description: Located on the beach in the vibrant Hastings neighborhood, the Coconut Court Beach Hotel provides reasonably priced lodging with breathtaking views of the ocean. The hotel offers free water sports, a restaurant on the beach, a swimming pool, and cozy accommodations.

2. Hotel Rostrevor:
Location: Christ Church, St. Lawrence Gap
- Price: $80 per night and up
The Rostrevor Hotel, which is centrally located in St. Lawrence Gap, provides affordable lodging that is close to dining options, retail establishments, and entertainment venues. The hotel offers close access to Dover Beach, a restaurant, a pool, and self-catering flats and apartments.

3. The Pirates Inn
- Site: Christ Church, Hastings
- Price: $70 per night and above
- Description: Situated close to the well-liked Accra Beach, Pirates Inn is an affordable lodging option. The hotel has convenient access to eating, shopping, and entertainment venues, as well as cozy rooms and apartments with kitchenettes, a swimming pool, and restaurant.

4. Melbourne Hotel:
- Site: Christ Church, Worthing
- Price: $60 per night and up
Melbourne Inn is a pleasant low-cost motel that is close to Worthing Beach. The hotel provides reasonably priced lodging with standard features including cable TV, Wi-Fi, and air conditioning. The beach and other nearby attractions are easily accessible on foot for visitors to enjoy the peaceful surroundings.

Mid-Scale Budget

1. Hotel South Gap:
Location: Christ Church, St. Lawrence Gap
- Price: $150 per night and up
- Description: Located in the vibrant St. Lawrence Gap neighborhood, the South Gap Hotel provides contemporary lodging with breathtaking ocean views. The hotel offers convenient access to beaches, restaurants, and nightlife, as well as large apartments and suites with a rooftop pool and restaurant.

2. Resort Divi Southwinds Beach:
Location: Christ Church, St. Lawrence Gap
- Price: $200 per night and above
- Description: Located on the beach, Divi Southwinds Beach Resort offers roomy apartments and condos with fully functional kitchens. The resort offers water sports, a restaurant, a fitness center, and three swimming pools. For families and couples looking for a cozy vacation with resort facilities, this is a great option.

3. Resort and Residences at Ocean Two:
- Site: Christ Church, Dover
- Price: $250 per night and up
- Description: Situated on Dover Beach, Ocean Two Resort and Residences is a boutique hotel that provides chic lodgings with contemporary conveniences. The hotel offers free water sports, a restaurant, a beachfront bar, a rooftop pool, and roomy apartments with views of the ocean.

4. Hotel Yellow Bird:

Location: Christ Church, St. Lawrence Gap
- Price: $180 per night and up
- Description: Located in the center of St. Lawrence Gap, the Yellow Bird Hotel is a delightful boutique hotel. The hotel has a rooftop pool, café, and panoramic views of the Caribbean Sea in addition to roomy apartments and suites with kitchenettes. Access to restaurants, entertainment, and beaches is convenient for visitors.

Luxurious

1. Sandy Lane Hotel:
Place: Parish of St. James
- Price: $1,000 per night and up
The Sandy Lane Hotel is an opulent resort situated on Barbados' esteemed western coast. The hotel has opulent rooms and suites, three golf courses, a top-notch spa, a number of dining options, swimming pools, and exclusive beach access.

2. The Resort at Crane:
Crane, St. Philip Parish is the location.
- Price: $500 per night and up
With a view of one of the greatest beaches in the world, Crane Beach, The Crane Resort is a luxurious hotel with a rich history. The resort has a spa, many dining options, infinity pools, luxury suites and private villas, and access to a breathtaking beachfront location.

3. Club Coral Reef:
Place: Parish of St. James

- Price: $600 per night and up
- Description: Located on Barbados' west coast, Coral Reef Club is a posh boutique hotel surrounded by tropical gardens. In a tranquil seaside location, the hotel offers opulent rooms and villas, award-winning restaurants, a spa, swimming pools, and individual service.

4. The luxurious resort and residences in Saint Peter's Bay:
Location: St. Peter Parish, Speightstown
- Price: $800 per night and up
The large beachfront suites at Saint Peter's Bay Luxury Resort and Residences provide stunning views of the Caribbean Sea. For an opulent stay, the resort offers opulent apartments with private plunge pools, a beach club, an infinity pool, a restaurant, and concierge services.

These hotels provide a variety of lodging options to accommodate various spending limits and tastes, guaranteeing a pleasurable and cozy stay in Barbados. Season, kind of lodging, and availability all affect prices, so it's better to book in advance to get the best deals.

Barbados' Best Restaurant

Low Spending
1. Cuz's Fish Market:
- Site: Bridgetown
- Price: $5 to $15 per individual
- Description: Cuz's Fish Shack is a well-liked location in Bridgetown for reasonably priced and mouthwatering seafood. This laid-back restaurant, which is close to the fishing harbor, offers perfectly grilled fresh fish, shrimp,

and lobster along with sides like macaroni pie or rice and peas. Both residents and visitors love it for its relaxed ambiance and welcoming staff.

2. Restaurant Peggy's Cove:
- Site: Christ Church, Rockley
- Price: $10 to $20 per individual
- Synopsis: Peggy's Cove Restaurant provides reasonably priced, traditional Bajan food. This welcoming eatery in Rockley offers both foreign classics and robust fare like pepperpot stew, cou-cou, and flying fish. Peggy's Cove, with its laid-back vibe and big quantities, is a fantastic option for a cheap supper in Barbados.

3. Simply Grilling:
- Place: St. James Parish, Holetown
- Price: $10 to $25 per individual
- Description: Just Grillin' is a laid-back eatery renowned for its mouthwatering grilled food and reasonable costs. This well-liked restaurant in Holetown serves grilled chicken, fish, burgers, and ribs along with delicious sides like coleslaw and fries. Both residents and tourists adore it because of the laid-back atmosphere and welcoming service.

4. Cheapside Café:
- Site: Bridgetown
- Price: $5 to $15 per individual
- Description: Serving affordable Bajan and Caribbean food, Cheapside Café is a hidden treasure in Bridgetown. This straightforward restaurant, which is situated in the

busy Cheapside Market, offers reasonably priced, filling fare including fried fish, rice and peas, and macaroni pie. Taste real food in a relaxed setting at Cheapside Café.

Mid-Scale Budget:

1. Tapas:
- Site: Christ Church, Hastings
- Price: $20 to $40 per individual
- Description: Tapas is a well-known eatery with a wide selection of tapas meals and small plates with Spanish influences that is situated on Barbados' south coast. This chic restaurant, which is conveniently located in the center of Hastings, has a lively environment, inventive drinks, and a large menu of hot and cold tapas that are ideal for sharing with friends and family.

2. Live Lobster:
- Place: Bridgetown's Carlisle Bay
- Price: $30 to $60 per individual
- Description: Specializing on fresh seafood, especially lobster, Lobster Alive is a beachside eatery. This little restaurant, which is situated in Bridgetown on Carlisle Bay, has a laid-back vibe with breathtaking views of the ocean. Live music, grilled lobster, seafood platters, and Caribbean-inspired cuisine made using regional ingredients are all available to guests.

3. Champers Wine Bar & Restaurant:
- Site: Christ Church, Rockley

- Price: $30 to $60 per individual
- Description: Known for its creative food and sophisticated atmosphere, Champers Restaurant and Wine Bar is a waterfront dining destination. This award-winning restaurant, which is located outside of Rockley, has a wide selection of foreign meals, steaks, and seafood on its menu. It also has a sizable wine list and stunning views of the ocean.

4. Grill & Noodles with Lemongrass Flavor:
- Site: Bridgetown
- Price: $20 to $40 per individual
- Description: Specializing on Asian-inspired dishes with a Caribbean touch, Lemongrass Noodle Bar and Grill provides a distinctive eating experience in Bridgetown. This hip restaurant, which serves a varied menu of noodle dishes, stir-fries, and grilled meats, is situated in the center of the city and has a welcoming environment and inventive drinks.

Luxurious
1. Cliff's Restaurant:
- Address: St. James Parish, Derricks
- Price: $60–$150+ per individual
- Description: Situated on a cliff with a breathtaking view of the Caribbean Sea is the well-known fine dining restaurant, The Cliff Restaurant. This award-winning restaurant, which is located in Derricks, has a delicious menu of modern Caribbean food, a well-chosen wine selection, and flawless service. The Cliff is renowned for its spectacular sunset views and romantic atmosphere.

2. Cin Cin by the Water:
- Site: St. James Parish, Prospect
- Price: $50 to $100 per individual
- Description: Situated on Barbados' west coast, Cin Cin By The Sea is a classy eatery that specializes in fresh seafood dishes with a Mediterranean influence. Located in Prospect, this elegant restaurant offers a variety of creative meals made with ingredients that are found locally, as well as a beautiful dining area with spectacular views of the ocean.

3. The restaurant Tides:
- Place: St. James Parish, Holetown
- Price: $50 to $100 per individual
- Description: Known for its sophisticated atmosphere and inventive food, The Tides Restaurant is a posh dining spot in Holetown. This elegant restaurant, housed in a restored coral-stone mansion, serves up a diverse menu of foreign cuisine, including fresh seafood, steaks, and vegetarian selections, all while providing a classy setting with an ocean view.

4. Cliff Beach Club:
- Address: St. James Parish, Derricks
- Price: $60–$150+ per individual
- Description: Situated next to The Cliff Restaurant in Derricks, Cliff Beach Club is a stylish beachside restaurant and bar. This upscale dining establishment has magnificent ocean views, cozy sitting spaces, a variety of delectable food, creative drinks, and premium

wines, all in a laid-back but elegant ambiance. Cliff Beach Club offers its patrons an opulent dining experience while their toes are on the beach.

These eateries guarantee a memorable dining experience in Barbados by providing a wide variety of culinary delights to fit all budgets and preferences. Season, menu selection, and beverage preferences may all affect prices.

Barbados's Top Malls and Marketplaces

Low Spending
1. Pelican Craft Center:
- Site: Bridgetown
- Price: $ - $$
- Description: Offering a large selection of regionally produced crafts, trinkets, and artwork, Pelican Craft Centre is a bustling market close to the Bridgetown harbor. Visitors may taste Bajan snacks and delicacies and peruse kiosks offering handcrafted jewelry, ceramics, wood carvings, and textiles. It's an excellent spot to locate one-of-a-kind presents and mementos since prices are usually reasonable.

2. Market on the Cheapside:
- Site: Bridgetown
- Price: $ - $$
- Description: Offering a wide range of fresh fruit, spices, and local items, Cheapside Market is a busy market situated in the center of Bridgetown. Aside from crafts, apparel, and mementos, visitors may peruse kiosks

offering fruits, veggies, spices, and handmade preserves. Bargaining is prevalent and prices are reasonable, making it a popular destination for both residents and visitors.

3. The Sheraton Mall
- Site: Christ Church
- Price: $ - $$
- Description: With a variety of retail stores, boutiques, and restaurants, Sheraton Mall is a well-liked shopping destination on Barbados' south coast. In addition to shopping for apparel, accessories, gadgets, and home items, visitors may have a bite to eat at one of the mall's eateries or food courts. There are alternatives for any budget, with prices varying based on the goods and shop.

4. Farmers Market in Hastings:
- Site: Christ Church, Hastings
- Price: $ - $$
- Description: Located in the Hastings neighborhood, the Hastings Farmers Market is a weekly market that offers a wide selection of handcrafted items, artisanal cuisine, and locally produced fruit. Shoppers may purchase baked foods, preserves, handcrafted crafts, and fresh fruits, vegetables, herbs, and spices. The market has affordable prices and a relaxed environment that makes it ideal for leisurely shopping and browsing.

Mid-Scale Budget
1. Limegrove Lifestyle Center:

- Place: St. James Parish, Holetown
- Price: $$ - $$$
- Description: Offering a carefully chosen assortment of designer boutiques, specialty stores, and eating choices, Limegrove Lifestyle Centre is a top shopping destination situated in the affluent Holetown neighborhood. In addition to shopping for high-end clothing, jewelry, cosmetics, and home products, visitors may eat or sip cocktails at one of the cafés or restaurants in the complex. Prices range from moderate to expensive, appealing to a posh customer base.

2. Quayside Center:
- Site: Bridgetown
- Price: $$ - $$$
- Description: Offering a variety of retail outlets, dining options, and entertainment venues, Quayside Centre is a waterfront shopping complex situated in Bridgetown. Along with shopping for apparel, accessories, presents, and mementos, guests may take advantage of waterfront eating options that provide harbor views. The center has modest prices and a laid-back vibe that makes it ideal for leisurely eating and shopping.

3. Sky Mall:
Location: St. Michael Parish's Haggatt Hall
- Price: $$ - $$$
- Description: Situated in Haggatt Hall, Sky Mall is a contemporary shopping complex with a range of dining establishments, entertainment venues, and retail stores. In addition to shopping for clothing, electronics, home

products, and other items, visitors may dine at the mall's eateries and watch a movie. The mall offers a pleasant and enjoyable shopping experience at reasonable prices.

4. Shell Exhibition:
Location: St. Peter Parish, Speightstown
- Price: $$ - $$$
- Description: Handmade jewelry, gifts, and souvenirs fashioned from shells and natural materials are the specialty of Shell Gallery, a distinctive Speightstown store. Along with learning about the regional shell business and conservation initiatives, visitors may peruse an extensive assortment of shell jewelry, decorations, home décor, and artwork. The gallery provides a pleasant and genuine shopping experience at reasonable prices.

Luxurious

1. Bridgetown's Broad Street:
- Site: Bridgetown
- Price: $$$ - $$$$
- Description: Brimming with high-end boutiques, department stores, and duty-free shops, Broad Street in Bridgetown serves as Barbados' primary retail avenue. Along with shopping for designer products, jewelry, watches, and luxury clothing, visitors may tour the area's historical buildings and landmarks. Duty-free shopping gives discounts on expensive things like jewelry and gadgets, but the prices are still exorbitant.

2. Chattel Village Holetown:

- Place: St. James Parish, Holetown
- Price: $$$ - $$$$
- Summary:

The quaint retail area of Holetown Chattel area is home to boutiques, galleries, and artisan stores in typical Bajan chattel cottages. Along with shopping for one-of-a-kind handcrafted goods, artwork, and souvenirs, visitors may eat or have a snack at one of the village's cafés or eateries. Given the excellent caliber and level of workmanship of the products on offer, the prices are considerable.

3. Barbados Craft Village:
- Site: Bridgetown
- Price: $$$ - $$$$
- Description: Showcasing the creations of regional craftsmen and artisans, Barbados Craft Village is a commercial and cultural complex close to Bridgetown. In addition to seeing demonstrations of traditional Bajan crafts including weaving and pottery, visitors may peruse booths offering handcrafted items, artwork, jewelry, and mementos. Although the items are expensive, the purchase is worthwhile due to their exceptional quality and originality.

4. West Coast Shopping Center:
Location: St. Peter Parish, Speightstown
- Price: $$$ - $$$$
- Description: West Coast Mall is a posh shopping destination in Speightstown that has a fine assortment

of specialized stores, galleries, and boutiques. Along with exquisite eating and entertainment choices, visitors may shop for designer clothing, fine jewelry, artwork, and home décor. Costs are expensive because they serve a well-educated customer base looking for upscale products and experiences.

CHAPTER 1: BARBADOS'S TOP CULTURAL ATTRACTIONS

George Washington House

In Bridgetown, Barbados' Garrison Historic Area, stands the historic George Washington House. George Washington only ever visited this one residence outside of the US. During his short time on the island in 1751, the first President of the United States is given a fascinating peek into his life at the home.

Highlights

1. Explore the exquisitely restored 18th-century home with period furniture, antiques, and hands-on displays on the Historic House Tour. Insight regarding George Washington's visit to Barbados and the island's colonial past may be gained from knowledgeable advisors.

2. Discover the details of George Washington's journey to Barbados when he was only 19 years old. Learn how his experiences on the island shaped his opinions on slavery, agriculture, and government, and how this affected his life and presidency.

3. Explore the Slave Quarters to learn about the life of those who were held as slaves during the colonial period and how they were used on the land. The house explores the complicated history of slavery in Barbados and its effects on the island's society via displays and educational activities.

4. Botanical Garden: Take leisurely strolls amid the tropical flora, blooming trees, and tranquil walkways that encircle George Washington House. Take in the serene surroundings while discovering the abundance of wildlife on the island.

5. Educational Programs: For guests of all ages, including school groups, families, and history buffs, George Washington House provides educational programs and seminars. George Washington's

biography, slavery, and colonial history are among the subjects covered in the programs.

Estimated Cost
- Adult admission to George Washington House normally costs between $10 and $20 USD; children, seniors, and organizations may get reduced prices.
- Additional costs for guided excursions may apply, based on the itinerary and length.
- There can be additional fees for special events and educational programs, so it's best to find out about them in advance of your visit.

Important Information for Travelers
- Location: George Washington House is just a short drive from the Barbados city center and popular tourist destinations. It is situated in the Garrison Historic Area of Bridgetown.
- Operating Hours: Guided tours are offered everyday from 9:00 AM to 4:30 PM, during which time the home is accessible to tourists. For the most recent information on opening hours and tour schedules, it is recommended that you visit the official website or get in touch with the home directly.
- Accessibility: With ramps and paved roads all over the property, the home and botanical garden are accessible to guests with mobility limitations. Upon request, guided tours may provide accommodations for those with special needs.
- Facilities: George Washington House features gift shops, restrooms, and a visitor center where visitors may

buy tickets and find out about future events, educational opportunities, and guided tours.

One of America's founding fathers' perspective of Barbados' rich history may be gained by traveling back in time to see George Washington House. Regardless of your interest in history, the outdoors, or the island's colonial past, a visit to George Washington House is sure to be enlightening and unforgettable.

Barbados Museum and Historical Society

Situated in Bridgetown, Barbados' Garrison Historic Area, is the cultural institution known as the Barbados Museum and Historical Society. Located in a former military jail that dates back to the 1800s, the museum provides visitors with a thorough understanding of Barbados' history, culture, and legacy.

Highlights
1. Look around the museum's permanent displays, which provide information on a variety of subjects like pre-Columbian history, colonization, slavery, emancipation, and independence. Highlights include multimedia exhibits that vividly depict Barbados' rich history together with relics, papers, and photos.

2. Explore the museum's historic structure, which was a military jail during the era of British colonization. The

architecture and design of the structure shed light on the island's history as a colony and its involvement in the transatlantic slave trade.

3. Special Exhibitions: The museum often holds temporary exhibits and special exhibitions that highlight certain facets of Barbados' past, present, and culture.

Visitors have the opportunity to interact with fresh viewpoints, creative interpretations, and research via these displays.

4. Explore Barbados' pre-Columbian history with the help of the museum's large archeological holdings. Ancient Arawak and Carib artifacts provide light on the ancestors of the island's population and way of life.

5. Programs for Education: The museum provides seminars and guided tours along with lectures and interactive activities for guests of all ages. The protection of cultural heritage, conservation, and archeology are among the subjects covered in the programs.

Estimated Cost
- Adult admission to the Barbados Museum and Historical Society normally costs between $10 and $20 USD; children, seniors, and groups may enter for less.
- Different entry prices apply to special exhibits and temporary shows; thus, it is best to check about exact charges before making travel arrangements.
- Additional costs for guided tours and educational programs may apply, based on the package and length.

Important Information for Travelers
- Location: The Barbados Museum and Historical Society is situated in Bridgetown, Barbados's Garrison Historic Area, just a short drive from the island's capital and popular tourist destinations.

- Operating Hours: Monday through Friday, 9:00 AM to 5:00 PM, with extended hours on some days and during special events, the museum is available to visitors. For the most recent details on special exhibits and opening hours, it is recommended to visit the official website or get in touch with the museum directly.
- Accessibility: The museum has ramps, elevators, and accessible bathrooms spread throughout the structure, making its amenities accessible to anyone with mobility disabilities. Upon request, guided tours may provide accommodations for those with special needs.
- Facilities: The Barbados Museum and Historical Society features a café where guests may buy food and drinks, as well as gift shops and restrooms.

St. Nicholas Abbey

In Barbados' St. Peter parish is the old plantation home known as St. Nicholas Abbey. Constructed in the middle of the 17th century, this home is among the oldest and best-preserved Jacobean structures on the island. With its breathtaking architecture, verdant grounds, and rich legacy, it provides tourists with a window into Barbados' colonial history.

Highlights

1. Take a tour of the exquisitely restored Great House, which has period furniture, ancient relics, and 17th and 18th century architectural aspects. Insight into the history of the home, its previous occupants, and the island's sugar economy may be gained from knowledgeable guides.

2. grounds Surrounding: St. Nicholas Abbey is surrounded by beautiful grounds with tropical plants, blooming trees, and peaceful walkways. Highlights include a set of medieval ruins, a tropical forest, and a charming gully.

3. Learn about the craft of making rum at the on-site distillery at St. Nicholas Abbey, which uses age-old techniques to create small-batch rum. In addition to tasting the estate's renowned rum, visitors may take a tour of the distillery and see the maturing barrels.

4. Discover more about Barbados' colonial past and its emphasis on sugar production at the Historic Plantation. Exhibits and educational activities at St. Nicholas Abbey delve into the life of enslaved workers on the estate and the economic effects of sugar cane on the island.

5. vintage train: Take a beautiful ride through the estate's gardens on St. Nicholas Abbey's vintage train. The train offers sweeping views of the surrounding landscape and a distinctive viewpoint on the cultural legacy and natural beauty of Barbados.

Estimated Cost
- Adult admission to St. Nicholas Abbey normally costs $20 to $40 USD, with group, senior, and child discounts available.
- Depending on the package and length, guided tours of the Great House and rum distillery may incur extra costs.
- Special activities might have different prices, so it's best to find out about exact fees before making travel arrangements. Examples of these events include rum tastings, vintage train trips, and cultural performances.

Important Information for Travelers

- Location: Bridgetown and other popular tourist destinations on the west coast are about a 30-minute drive away from St. Nicholas Abbey, which is situated in St. Peter Parish, Barbados.
- Operating Hours: The estate is open to guests every day from 10:00 AM to 3:30 PM. All day long, there are guided tours and activities to enjoy. The best way to find out the most recent details on opening times and tour schedules is to visit the official website or get in touch with St. Nicholas Abbey privately.
- Accessibility: St. Nicholas Abbey's Great House and grounds are handicapped-accessible, with paved walkways and ramps available for guests with mobility issues. Upon request, guided tours may provide accommodations for those with special needs.
- Facilities: St. Nicholas Abbey contains a café where guests may buy food and beverages, as well as restrooms and a gift store. For visitors arriving by automobile or rental car, on-site parking is provided.

A rare chance to go back in time and take in the beauty and splendor of Barbados' colonial history is to visit St. Nicholas Abbey. A visit to St. Nicholas Abbey promises to be instructive, enjoyable, and unforgettable—whether you're a history buff, a connoisseur of rum, or just looking for a peaceful getaway among beautiful gardens and old buildings.

Nidhe Israel Synagogue and Museum

One of the oldest synagogues in the Western Hemisphere is the Nidhe Israel Synagogue and Museum, which is situated in Bridgetown, Barbados. The synagogue, which was constructed in 1654 by Sephardic Jews who were fleeing persecution in Brazil, is evidence of Barbados' rich religious and cultural history.

Highlights

1. Explore the historic synagogue, which has distinctive architectural characteristics that honor the congregation's Sephardic background, a sand-covered floor, and lovely architecture. Discover the background of Judaism in Barbados as well as the synagogue's significance to the religious and cultural life of the island.

2. Jewish Museum: Explore the museum next to the synagogue, which has artifacts, records, and images that chronicle the history of the Jewish community in Barbados. Highlights include religious artifacts, ceremonial objects, and historical documents that provide light on Barbadian Jews' way of life and customs.

3. Burial Ground: Take a tour of the nearby Jewish cemetery, one of the oldest in the Western Hemisphere and dating back to the 17th century. Honor the pioneers and local authorities buried here, and discover the things they contributed to Barbados culture.

4. Educational Programs: For visitors of all ages, including school groups, families, and history buffs, the Nidhe Israel Synagogue and Museum provides guided tours and educational programs. Programs include subjects including Barbados' pluralism, historical preservation, and Jewish history.

Estimated Cost

- Adult admission to the Nidhe Israel Synagogue and Museum normally costs between $10 and $15 USD; children, seniors, and organizations may get reduced prices.
- Depending on the package and length, guided tours of the cemetery, museum, and synagogue may incur extra costs.
- Special events, such religious services, talks, and plays, could have different prices, so it's a good idea to find out about the details in advance of your visit.

Important Information for Travelers
- Location: The Nidhe Israel Synagogue and Museum is situated in Bridgetown, Barbados, close to the city center and other popular tourist destinations.
- Operating Hours: Guided tours and displays are offered all day long, and the synagogue and museum are accessible to tourists on weekdays from 9:00 AM to 4:00 PM. To ensure you get the most recent details on opening hours and tour itineraries, visit the official website or get in touch with the synagogue directly.
- Accessibility: There are ramps and accessible facilities provided to make the synagogue and museum accessible to anyone with mobility limitations. Upon request, guided tours may provide accommodations for those with special needs.
- Facilities: There are restrooms, a gift store, and a small café where guests may buy food and beverages at the Nidhe Israel Synagogue and Museum. There is parking close by for anyone arriving by car or rental car.

Discovering the rich historical and cultural legacy of Barbados' Jewish community can be done only by going to the Nidhe Israel Synagogue and Museum.

Bridgetown and its Historic Garrison

Barbados' capital city is home to Bridgetown and its Historic Garrison, a UNESCO World Heritage Site. This historic region is made up of a diverse array of military fortifications, colonial architecture, and cultural relics that all contribute to the rich history and legacy of the island.

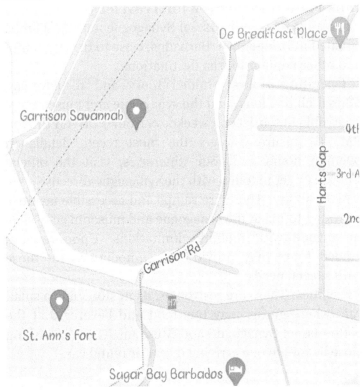

Highlights

1. Visit the ancient Parliament Buildings, one of the oldest governmental buildings in the Caribbean and home to the Parliament of Barbados. The neo-Gothic architecture, the Lord Nelson monument, and the old Chamberlain Bridge are among the attractions.

2. Discover National Heroes Square, originally known as Trafalgar Square, the center of civic and cultural activities in Bridgetown. The famous Jubilee Gardens, the Lord Nelson Statue, and the Cenotaph War Memorial are all located in the plaza.

3. Explore the Historic Garrison Area, a UNESCO World Heritage Site that consists of a collection of 17th and 18th-century military fortifications, barracks, and historic buildings. The George Washington House, the Barbados Museum, and a number of old forts and batteries are among the area's highlights.

4. One of the oldest British forts in the Caribbean, Charles Fort provides sweeping views over Carlisle Bay and Bridgetown. The fort's subterranean tunnels, cannons, and well-preserved walls provide light on Barbados' strategic significance and colonial history.

5. Discover St. Ann's Garrison, a former British military installation that is currently the location of the George Washington House, the Barbados Museum, and the Barbados Defence Force Headquarters. There are also

walking routes, historic monuments, and verdant gardens in the Garrison neighborhood.

Estimated Cost
The cost of admission varies depending on the attraction; certain parts of Bridgetown and its Historic Garrison are free to enter, while others have a charge.
- Additional costs may apply for guided tours of certain locations or landmarks, based on the package and length.
- Special events, such festivals, reenactments, and cultural performances, could have different prices, so it's best to find out about exact rates before making travel arrangements.

Important Information for Travelers
- Location: Situated in Barbados' capital city, Bridgetown and its Historic Garrison are easily accessible by foot from the island's top tourist destinations, lodging facilities, and cruise ship ports.
- Hours of Operation: Each attraction in the Historic Garrison Area has a different set of hours; some are open everyday to tourists, while others are closed on certain days of the week. The best way to find out the most recent details on opening times and tour schedules is to visit the official websites or get in touch with the attractions directly.
- Accessibility: With ramps, elevators, and accessible facilities available, many of Bridgetown's attractions, including its Historic Garrison, are accessible to guests with mobility disabilities. Upon request, guided tours

may provide accommodations for those with special needs.

- Facilities: Restrooms, tourist centers, gift shops, and cafés where guests may buy snacks and mementos are all available in the Historic Garrison Area. There is parking close by for anyone arriving by car or rental car.

Discovering Barbados' rich history, culture, and tradition can be done only by visiting Bridgetown and its Historic Garrison. A visit to Bridgetown and its Historic Garrison is sure to be instructive, illuminating, and unforgettable, regardless of your interests in colonial architecture, military history, or just wanting to take in the island's rich cultural environment.

CHAPTER 2: THE BEST NATURAL ATTRACTIONS IN BARBADOS

Hunte's Gardens

Nestled within verdant hills of St. Joseph parish, Barbados, is a botanical haven known as Hunte's

Gardens. Anthony Hunte, a horticulturist, created the gardens, which provide guests with a tranquil getaway into a tropical dream with colorful flowers, exotic plants, and winding walkways.

Highlights

1. Discover the wide variety of tropical flowers and plants that grow at Hunte's Gardens by exploring the Tropical Flora. Highlights include carefully chosen

exotic plants from all over the globe, such as bromeliads, orchids, palms, ferns, and other plants, which combine to produce a breathtaking display of color and texture.

2. Wander along the exquisitely designed paths that meander through the gardens, taking you past peaceful lounging places, bubbling brooks, and secret grottos. The paths allow for quiet contemplation and relaxation while providing stunning views of the surrounding landscape.

3. Natural Grotto: Tucked away in the grounds, this undiscovered treasure acts as a center of attention for guests. Tropical greenery, tumbling vines, and trickling water features surround the grotto, creating a mystical ambiance that transports guests to a another realm.

4. Birdwatching: With a wide range of resident and migratory bird species, Hunte's Gardens is a birdwatcher's paradise. It's a nature lover's heaven, with vibrant birds like hummingbirds, finches, and bananaquits flying among the trees and flowers.

5. Admire the creative details found throughout Hunte's Gardens, such as the statues, sculptures, and ornamental pieces that meld well with the surrounding landscape. The feeling of awe and discovery is enhanced by the fresh creative surprise that is revealed around every corner of the gardens.

Estimated Cost

- Adult admission to Hunte's Gardens normally costs between $15 and $25 USD; children, seniors, and organizations may pay less.
- Depending on the package and length, guided tours of the gardens may incur extra costs.
- Special events, such musical concerts, art exhibits, and garden parties, could have different prices, so it's best to find out about exact charges before making travel arrangements.

Important Information for Travelers
- Location: About a half-hour's drive from Bridgetown and other popular west coast tourist destinations, Hunte's Gardens is situated in the highlands of St. Joseph parish, Barbados.
- Operating Hours: Guided tours and activities are offered all day long, and the gardens are accessible to tourists every day from 9:00 AM to 5:00 PM. To get the most recent details on opening times and tour schedules, it is recommended that you visit the official website or get in touch with Hunte's Gardens directly.
- Accessibility: With ramps and concrete paths all across the grounds, Hunte's Gardens is accessible to guests with mobility limitations. Visitors with special requirements should, however, make plans for the possibility of rough ground or stairs in some places of the gardens.
- Facilities: Hunte's Gardens contains a café where guests may buy food and beverages, as well as restrooms and a gift store. For visitors arriving by automobile or rental car, on-site parking is provided.

It's a fantastic experience to visit Hunte's Gardens, where you may lose yourself in the peace and beauty of Barbados' natural surroundings. A visit to Hunte's Gardens is sure to be a wonderful and revitalizing experience, regardless of your interests—gardening, nature, or just finding a quiet haven among verdant surroundings.

Harrison's Cave

A natural marvel, Harrison's Cave is situated in Barbados' middle uplands. This limestone cavern is one of the most visited tourist destinations on the island because of its crystalline formations, subterranean streams, and stunning waterfalls.

Highlights

1. Tram Tours: Venture into the heart of Harrison's Cave with a tram tour that brings guests there. Stalactites, stalagmites, flowstones, and crystal-clear lakes are just a few of the amazing structures you'll see as you make your way through the cave's mazy passageways and chambers.

2. Admire the Crystal Pool, a breathtaking natural pool with crystal-clear, blue water that reflects the various formations within the cave and creates a mystical atmosphere. Photographs, hand dips in the refreshing water, and admiring this natural wonder's splendor are all available to visitors.

3. Waterfalls: The inside of the cave is punctuated by tumbling waterfalls, which provide a dramatic and engrossing ambiance. The strength and beauty of nature's powers may be appreciated by visitors who can go up close to the waterfalls and feel the mist on their skin.

4. Interactive exhibits and educational displays at Harrison's Cave's visitor center teach visitors about the geological development and historical background of the cave. Learn about the ecology that lives in the cave's depths and how it was developed over thousands of years.

5. Nature paths: Take a stroll along the paths that meander through verdant woods, picturesque gullies, and expansive vistas to discover the surrounding area of Harrison's Cave. The uplands of Barbados offer visitors hiking, birding, and picnicking opportunities among breathtaking natural scenery.

Estimated Cost
- Adult admission to Harrison's Cave normally costs between $25 and $40 USD, with group, senior, and child discounts available.
- Depending on the package and length, there can be extra costs for the cave tram trips.
- Exotic experiences, including photo courses, eco-adventures, and adventure tours, might have different prices, so it's best to find out about the charges before making travel arrangements.

Important Information for Travelers
- Location: Harrison's Cave is situated in Barbados' middle uplands, some thirty minutes' drive from Bridgetown and the island's main tourist destinations on the west coast.

- Operating Hours: Tram rides run everyday from 9:00 AM to 3:30 PM, during which time the cave is available to tourists. The best way to find out the most recent details about Harrison's Cave's opening times and tour schedules is to visit the official website or get in touch with them directly.
- Accessibility: Ramps, elevators, and accessible facilities are provided to make Harrison's Cave accessible to guests with mobility limitations. Upon request, tram trips may provide accommodations for those with special needs.
- Facilities: Harrison's Cave contains a café where guests may buy food and beverages, as well as restrooms and a gift store. For visitors arriving by automobile or rental car, on-site parking is provided.

Traveling to Harrison's Cave is a once-in-a-lifetime experience that immerses guests in Barbados' breathtaking scenery and geological marvels. Harrison's Cave is a must-visit location for anybody interested in wildlife, photography, or just having a unique experience. It's sure to be instructive, thrilling, and breathtaking.

Animal Flower Cave

Situated close to the community of North Point at the northern point of Barbados, is a natural sea cave known as the Animal Flower Cave. This geological wonder is well-known for its spectacular coastline landscape, tidal pools, and coral reef formations, which make it a popular tourist and outdoor recreation location.

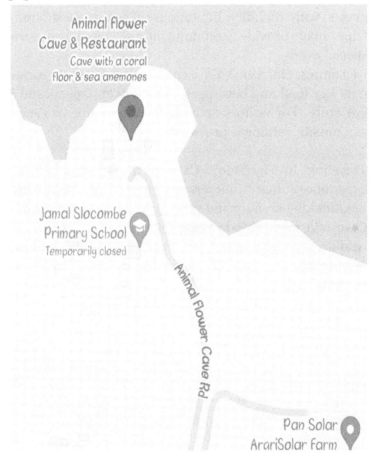

Highlights

1. Cave Exploration: Dive into the heart of the Animal Flower Cave to discover its vast halls, striking limestone structures, and glistening pools of saltwater. The natural beauty and geological marvels inside the cave may be marveled at by visitors as they meander through its twisting tunnels.

2. Ocean Views: From the cave's cliffside position, take in expansive views of the Atlantic Ocean that include crashing waves, rocky coastlines, and striking rock formations. A beautiful setting for leisure, reflection, and photography may be found in the Animal Flower Cave.

3. Tidal Pools: The natural tidal pools in the cave are a wonderful place to swim. They are brimming with marine life and have beautiful, blue water. In the pools, guests may swim, snorkel, or just wade to get up close and personal with colorful fish, sea anemones, and other aquatic life.

4. Explore the colorful coral reef that encircles the Animal Flower Cave, which is home to a wide variety of marine life and habitats. Divers and snorkelers may explore the underwater ecosystems of the reef and come across beautiful coral formations, tropical fish, and sea turtles.

5. Cliffside Restaurant: Enjoy fresh seafood, tropical beverages, and Caribbean cuisine while soaking in the

breathtaking ocean views at this laid-back eatery that is close to the Animal Flower Cave entrance. The restaurant is a great place to dine and mingle since it has both indoor and outdoor seating.

Estimated Cost
- Adult admission to the Animal Flower Cave normally costs between $10 and $20 USD; children, seniors, and groups may enter for less.
- Depending on the package and length, guided tours of the cave may incur extra costs.
- Masks, fins, and snorkels are among the equipment that may be rented for diving and snorkeling for an extra fee.

Important Information for Travelers
- Location: About a 45-minute drive from Bridgetown and other popular tourist destinations on the island's west coast, the Animal Flower Cave is situated near Barbados' northernmost point.
- Operating Hours: Daily from 9:00 AM to 4:30 PM, the cave is accessible to tourists. During the day, guided tours and attractions are offered. To ensure you get the most recent details on opening times and tour itineraries, visit the official website or get in touch with the Animal Flower Cave directly.
- Accessibility: Due to the rough terrain and steps leading to the cave, guests with mobility limitations may not be able to reach the Animal Flower Cave. When making travel plans, guests with special needs should enquire about accessible features and accommodations.

- Facilities: Visitors to the Animal Flower Cave may enjoy showers, changing rooms, and restrooms. For visitors arriving by automobile or rental car, on-site parking is provided.

Welchman Hall Gully

A natural landmark in Barbados' central parish of St. Thomas is Welchman Hall Gully. This unusual geological structure, a tropical wooded ravine with towering trees and a network of walking pathways, provides tourists with a peaceful natural retreat.

Highlights

1. Discover the wide variety of tropical trees and plants that abound in Welchman Hall Gully's tropical vegetation. Highlights include the lush and green scenery created by tall mahogany trees, magnificent palms, colorful floral plants, and unique ferns.

2. Walking routes: Guests may experience the natural beauty of Welchman Hall Gully at their own leisure by strolling along the network of walking routes that meander around the ravine. The paths provide peaceful settings for photography, animal observation, and birding.

3. Explore the historic elements scattered around Welchman Hall Gully, such as relics from the island's plantation past and its previous sugar cane industry. Old plantation ruins, sugar mill equipment, and other relics that provide light on Barbados' colonial history are available for exploration by tourists.

4. Observing animals: Welchman Hall Gully is home to a variety of animals, such as tiny mammals, green monkeys, and tropical birds. Birdwatchers will find the gully to be a sanctuary, since they may often observe hummingbirds, warblers, and bananaquits among the vegetation.

5. Educational Exhibits: At the gully's visitor center, discover the natural history and ecological importance of Welchman Hall Gully via interpretive exhibits and

educational displays. Learn about the formation of the gully, its significance to Barbados' ecology, and the current initiatives to conserve and maintain its biodiversity.

Estimated Cost
- Adult admission to Welchman Hall Gully normally costs between $10 and $15 USD; children, seniors, and organizations may enter for less.
- Depending on the package and length, guided tours of the gully could incur extra costs.
- Special activities, including photography workshops, birding excursions, and guided nature walks, could have different prices, so it's best to find out about them in advance of your visit.

Important Information for Travelers
- Location: Bridgetown and other popular west coast tourist destinations are about a 30-minute drive from Welchman Hall Gully, which is situated in the center parish of St. Thomas, Barbados.
- Operating Hours: Walking paths are available all day long, and the gully is open to tourists every day from 9:00 AM to 4:00 PM. To get the most recent information on trail conditions and operating hours, it is recommended to visit the official website or get in touch with Welchman Hall Gully directly.
- Accessibility: Due to the uneven walkways and stairs around the area, Welchman Hall Gully may not be accessible to guests with mobility difficulties. When

making travel plans, guests with special needs should enquire about accessible features and accommodations.
- Amenities: Welchman Hall Gully includes a café where guests may buy food and drinks, a gift store, and restrooms. For visitors arriving by automobile or rental car, on-site parking is provided.

CHAPTER 3: BEACHES AND WATER SPORTS

Bottom Bay

Barbados's southeast coast is home to the lovely beach known as Bottom Bay. Tourists looking for a quiet and peaceful beach experience often visit Bottom Bay because of its breathtaking natural beauty, pristine white beaches, and striking cliffs.

Highlights

1. Scenic Beauty: Bask in the stunning blue seas, snow-white beaches, and towering limestone cliffs that define Bottom Bay's natural beauty. The beach is surrounded by thick flora and waving palm trees, giving the area a picture-perfect tropical setting.

2. isolated Atmosphere: Bottom Bay is well known for its quiet and isolated atmosphere. Come here to escape the throng and take in the solitude. In a tranquil and picturesque environment, guests may relax on the immaculate dunes, go swimming in the quiet waters, or just soak up the sun.

3. Surfing and Bodyboarding: At Bottom Bay, where the waves sweep in, water sports lovers may enjoy the exhilaration of surfing or bodyboarding. The beach is well-liked by bodyboarders and surfers of all abilities, providing possibilities for both novices and pro riders.

4. Relaxation & Picnicking: Head to Bottom Bay for a day of leisurely relaxation. The area's grassy lawns and shaded picnic spaces provide for ideal settings for a leisurely lunch or afternoon siesta. Unpack a picnic basket, throw out a blanket, and relax in the beach's unspoiled splendor.

5. Sunrise and Sunset: At Bottom Bay, take in the breathtaking dawn or sunset as the beach is bathed in a mystical light and the sky bursts into a blaze of vivid hues. Great times for photography, meditation, and romantic walks along the coast are in the early morning and late afternoon.

Estimated Cost
- Bottom Bay is an inexpensive tourist spot since there is no entry charge.
- In order to travel from their lodging to Bottom Bay, visitors may need to factor in additional expenses for transportation, such as taxi charges or rental vehicle fees.

Important Information for Travelers
- Location: Bridgetown and other popular tourist destinations on the west coast of Barbados are about a 30-minute drive away from Bottom Bay, which is situated on the island's southeast coast.
- Access: There is a small route from the main road that leads to Bottom Bay, and parking is provided for tourists. Visitors with limited mobility should make appropriate plans since the route leads down steps to the beach.
- Facilities: Since Bottom Bay doesn't have a lot of amenities, guests should pack light and bring beach towels, drinks, sunscreen, and snacks. Since there are no lifeguards on duty, swimmers should use care, particularly in choppy waves.

- Local Advice: Because Bottom Bay is notorious for its powerful currents and choppy waves, it's best to swim in approved locations and pay attention to any warning signs that are placed along the shore. Visitors should also be aware of their possessions and refrain from leaving expensive items unsecured while enjoying the beach.

Immersion in the natural beauty and peacefulness of Barbados' shoreline may be had at Bottom Bay, making it a remarkable experience. Bottom Bay guarantees an amazing beach experience, whether you're looking for adventure, relaxation, or just a gorgeous background for your holiday pictures.

Crane Beach

On Barbados' southeast coast is a famous stretch of shoreline known as Crane Beach. Crane Beach, well-known for its fluffy pink sand, turquoise waves, and breathtaking coastline panoramas, is often listed by travel journals and experts as one of the best beaches in the world.

Highlights
1. Pink Sand: Be amazed by the distinctive pink color of the sand at Crane Beach, which is caused by the inclusion of shells and crushed coral. The sand is perfect for sunbathing, beachcombing, and making sandcastles because of its soft, powdery texture.

2. Surfing and Bodyboarding: Crane Beach offers great conditions for water sports lovers to enjoy the exhilaration of surfing or bodyboarding due to its rolling waves. All skill levels of surfers and bodyboarders use the beach, which has waves that are easier for novices to ride as well as more difficult ones for more experienced riders.

3. Natural Beauty: Bask in the stunning natural beauty of Crane Beach, which is surrounded by lush tropical flora, towering limestone cliffs, and swinging coconut palms. Swimming, tanning, and beach sports are beautifully framed by the craggy shoreline and striking rock formations.

4. Swimming and Snorkeling: Crane Beach has crystal-clear, turquoise waters that are ideal for swimmers of all ages and skill levels due to its mild waves and shallow entrance. Enjoy a revitalizing swim there. Exploring the colorful coral reefs and marine creatures that flourish along the beach is possible for snorkeling aficionados.

5. Luxurious Amenities: Crane Beach provides guests with a variety of opulent amenities and facilities so they may unwind in style. The historic Crane Resort is located on the beach, offering visitors cabanas, umbrellas, and beachside loungers in addition to on-site dining options, drinking establishments, and spa facilities.

Estimated Cost
- Because Crane Beach is free to enter, travelers may afford to visit this reasonably priced location.
- For an additional charge, visitors staying at the Crane Resort may have access to extra features and services such beachside loungers, umbrellas, and watersports equipment rentals.

Important Information for Travelers
- Location: Bridgetown and other popular tourist destinations on the west coast of Barbados are about a 30-minute drive from Crane Beach, which is situated on the island's southeast coast.
- Access: From the Crane Resort, where parking is accessible, tourists may reach Crane Beach by a short trail. Visitors with limited mobility should make appropriate plans since the route leads down steps to the beach.
- Facilities: Crane Beach provides tourists with showers, changing rooms, and restrooms. There may be more facilities available to Crane Resort visitors, such cabanas, umbrellas, and beach loungers.
- Safety: Although swimming at Crane Beach is usually safe, guests should use care, particularly when there are strong currents or choppy waves. Swimmers should stay in specified zones and pay attention to any caution signs put on the beach since lifeguards are not always on duty.

Any traveler to Barbados should make time to explore Crane Beach, which offers the ideal fusion of recreational opportunities, natural beauty, and opulent comforts. Crane Beach guarantees an amazing beach experience, whether you're looking for adventure, relaxation, or just a gorgeous background for your holiday pictures.

Accra Beach (Rockley Beach)

On Barbados' southern coast, Accra Beach—also called Rockley Beach—is a well-liked and energetic beach. Accra Beach is a well-liked hangout for sun, sea, and relaxation for both residents and visitors due to its smooth white sand, azure seas, and vibrant ambience.

Highlights

1. Swimming and Snorkeling: Take advantage of Accra Beach's serene, pristine waters for swimming and snorkeling. Families and novices will find it the perfect place to wade and discover the underwater marine life and coral reefs because of the mild waves and shallow entrance.

2. Water Sports: Enjoy a variety of water sports at Accra Beach, like as kayaking, paddleboarding, and jet skiing. Adventuresome tourists may explore the shoreline or try out thrilling water activities by renting equipment from local sellers.

3. Beach facilities: Accra Beach offers a variety of facilities for your convenience while you relax on the powder-soft white sand. In addition to merchants offering food, beverages, and mementos, beachgoers may hire beach chairs, umbrellas, and sun loungers.

4. Dining & Entertainment: Accra Beach is lined with beachside restaurants and bars where you can savor delectable Caribbean food. Savor freshly caught seafood, lively tropical drinks, and live music while taking in the lively ambiance and breathtaking views of the ocean.

5. Wander down Accra Beach's beachfront for a romantic walk as the sun sets, allowing you to take in the golden colors of the setting sun and the soft touch of the wind on your skin. It's the ideal way to cap off a day of leisurely sunbathing.

Estimated Cost
- Since everyone may access Accra Beach for free, it's an affordable travel destination.
It may be necessary for guests to factor in extra expenses for things like gear rentals, beach chair and umbrella rentals, and vendor purchases.

Important Information for Travelers
- Location: Bridgetown and other popular tourist destinations on Barbados' west coast are about a 15-minute drive from Accra Beach, which is on the island's southern shore.
- Access: Parking is close by, and Accra Beach is just a short stroll from the main road. There are bus stations close by so you may take public transit to the beach.
- Facilities: Visitors to Accra Beach may enjoy showers, changing rooms, and restrooms. Additionally, there are eateries, pubs, and cafés beside the beach where guests may buy food, beverages, and snacks.
- Safety: Although swimming at Accra Beach is usually safe, tourists should use care, particularly when there are strong currents or choppy waves. Swimmers should stay in specified zones and pay attention to any caution

signs put on the beach since lifeguards are not always on duty.

Accra Beach is a wonderful destination that provides the ideal fusion of leisure, recreation, and Caribbean charm. For those looking for excitement, adventure, or just a relaxing day by the water, Accra Beach guarantees to provide an amazing beach experience for all ages.

Carlisle Bay

Barbados' southwest coast is home to the breathtaking natural harbor known as Carlisle Bay. Carlisle Bay is well-liked by beachgoers, fans of water sports, and those who enjoy the great outdoors because of its pristine blue seas, powdery white beaches, and abundant marine life.

Highlights

1. Snorkeling and diving: Discover the rich underwater environment of Carlisle Bay, which is home to a variety of marine organisms as well as shipwrecks and coral reefs. Just a short distance from the coast, snorkelers and divers may see vibrant fish, sea turtles, and intriguing undersea structures.

2. Water Sports: Enjoy a variety of water sports in Carlisle Bay, such as kayaking, paddleboarding, and jet skiing. Adventuresome guests may explore the bay's tranquil waters or try their hand at thrilling water sports by renting equipment from local merchants.

3. Beachfront Dining: At the beachside eateries and bars that line Carlisle Bay, savor delectable Caribbean food. Savor freshly caught seafood, lively music, and tropical drinks while taking in the laid-back ambiance and breathtaking views of the ocean.

4. Historic monuments: Learn about the cultural monuments and historic sites, such as the Barbados Garrison, George Washington House, and the Barbados Museum, that are close to Carlisle Bay. History enthusiasts may discover more about Barbados' rich colonial history and cultural legacy by visiting these locations.

5. Sunset Cruises: Savor the stunning vistas of the Caribbean Sea as the sun sets on a romantic sunset boat around Carlisle Bay. After a day of lounging on the beach, several tour companies offer sunset cruises that include food, cocktails, and live entertainment.

Estimated Cost
- Carlisle Bay is an inexpensive travel destination since it is open to all visitors for free.
It may be necessary for guests to factor in extra expenses for things like gear rentals, beach chair and umbrella rentals, and vendor purchases.
- It's a good idea to ask about precise charges when making a reservation since activities like guided snorkeling excursions and sunset cruises could have different prices.

Important Information for Travelers
- Location: Bridgetown and other popular tourist destinations on the west coast are around ten minutes' drive from Carlisle Bay, which is situated on Barbados' southwest coast.
- Access: Parking is close by, and walking from the main road to Carlisle Bay is a short walk. There are bus stations close by so you may take public transit to the beach.

- Facilities: Carlisle Bay provides guests with showers, changing rooms, and restrooms. Additionally, there are eateries, pubs, and cafés beside the beach where guests may buy food, beverages, and snacks.
- Safety: Although swimming and water sports in Carlisle Bay are usually safe, visitors should nevertheless use care, particularly at times of high waves or strong currents. Swimmers should stay in specified zones and pay attention to any caution signs put on the beach since lifeguards are not always on duty.

Carlisle Bay is a unique destination that has something to offer everyone, from sightseeing and snorkeling to tanning and leisure. For those looking for excitement, adventure, or just a relaxing day by the water, Carlisle Bay promises to provide a memorable beach experience for everyone.

CHAPTER 4: FOOD AND DRINKS

Barbados 's Cocktail Tour

Take a pleasant tour of Barbados' lively cocktail scene, where rum is king and tropical tastes are abundant. During the Barbados Cocktail Tour, guests may enjoy a variety of specialty cocktails made with ingredients that are obtained locally and imbued with the rich cultural legacy of the island.

Highlights

1. Rum Distillery Tours: Visit one of Barbados' well-known rum distilleries, such Mount Gay Rum Distillery or Foursquare Rum Distillery, to start your cocktail journey. Learn about the history of rum production on the island and the distillation process by taking a guided tour of the facilities.

2. Rum Punch: Begin your culinary adventure with the traditional beverage of Barbados, the rum punch. A tasty and pleasant drink that embodies Caribbean hospitality, rum punch is made with a mixture of rum, lime juice, sugar, and bitters. No two punches are the same since every bartender puts their own special spin on this traditional formula.

3. Flying Fish Rum Sour: Try this contemporary take on the classic sour drink, created with regional Bajan ingredients. This cool beverage is topped with a piece of fresh fruit and a sprig of mint and contains rum, sugar, fresh lime juice, and a dash of Angostura bitters.

4. Coconut Mojito: A creamy and delightful drink created with coconut rum, fresh mint, lime juice, coconut cream, and soda water, this concoction lets you indulge in the tropical tastes of Barbados. This refreshing beverage, served over ice and topped with a

lime wedge and a sprig of mint, is ideal for a hot Caribbean day.

5. Bajan Rum Runner: A delicious and tropical beverage composed with rum, banana liqueur, blackberry brandy, orange juice, and grenadine, this drink lets you experience the strong tastes of Barbados. This bright beverage is topped with crushed ice, vivid fresh fruit garnishes, and a cocktail umbrella.

Estimated Cost
- The number of locations visited, the kinds of beverages tasted, and any extra experiences or activities included in the trip package all affect how much the Barbados Cocktail trip costs.

Tastings may be free of charge or extra, and guided tours of rum distilleries may need supplementary entry costs.

Important Information for Travelers
- Booking: You may make direct reservations with participating venues, hotels, or tour operators for the Barbados Cocktail Tour. Making reservations in advance is advised, particularly during the busiest travel seasons.
- Transportation: Tour packages may include transportation between cocktail venues and rum distilleries, or guests may make their own travel arrangements via taxi or rental vehicle.
- Safety: During the cocktail tour, it's crucial to pace yourself and drink sensibly. Along the way, be sure to eat and drink enough of water to avoid overindulging. Never

drink and drive; instead, plan to designate a driver or use an other mode of transportation.

With a range of unique cocktails made with regional tastes and ingredients, the Barbados Cocktail Tour is a pleasant way to see the island's thriving cocktail culture. The Barbados Cocktail Tour looks to be a fun and unforgettable event for anybody interested in the Caribbean, rum enthusiasts, or sophisticated cocktail makers.

Barbados' Local Foods

African, European, and Caribbean cuisines have all affected Barbados' rich culinary legacy. These are some of the most well-liked regional dishes in Barbados, along with descriptions:

1. Cou Cou with Fish in the Air:
- Description: Cooked till thick and smooth, coucou is a classic Bajan dish made with cornmeal and okra. It is often served with flying fish, which is seasoned with Bajan spices and either steamed or fried. This meal is a mainstay of Bajan cuisine and is regarded as the national dish of Barbados.

2. Fish Cutter:
- Description: A fried fish fillet, usually mahi-mahi or marlin, sandwiched between two pieces of salt bread or a roll is called a "fish cutter," and it's a common street snack in Barbados. It makes a tasty and filling lunch

when topped with lettuce, tomato, and Bajan spicy sauce.

3. Macaroni pie from Bajan:
- Description: A delicious baked meal with a Bajan touch, Bajan Macaroni Pie is akin to macaroni & cheese. It has macaroni noodles combined with a thick, creamy cheese sauce prepared with milk, eggs, cheddar cheese, and Bajan flavors such as spicy sauce and mustard.

4. Souse and Pudding:
- Description: Souse and pudding is a classic Bajan meal that consists of sweet potato pudding with pickled pork (souse). While the pudding is prepared with grated sweet potatoes, flour, and spices and steam-cooked until firm, the pork is marinated in a blend of lime juice, vinegar, onions, and Bajan seasonings.

5. Conkies:
Conkies are a savory and sweet Bajan treat that's eaten in honor of Barbados Independence Day. Encased in banana leaves and steam-cooked, they are composed of a blend of cornmeal, coconut, pumpkin, sweet potato, raisins, and spices. Conkies have a distinct taste and texture with a touch of sweetness from the raisins and coconut.

6. Plantain fries:
- Description: Sliced ripe plantains are fried till golden brown and caramelized, making fried plantains a

popular side dish in Barbados. They have a crispy outside and a soft, sensitive inside that are both sweet and delicious. Fried plantains are often included with meals as a snack or side dish.

7. Black Cake from Bajan:
- Description: Served at Christmas and weddings, Bajan Black Cake, often called rum cake or fruit cake, is a rich and luscious treat. Dried fruits, including prunes, raisins, and currants, are combined with flour, eggs, butter, and spices after being soaked in rum. Because of the rum and spice infusion, the cake is rich, moist, and full of flavor.

8. Fish cakes & bakes:
- Description: A common Bajan breakfast or snack, bakes are a form of fried dough that resembles a bread roll and are sometimes eaten with fish cakes. Fish cakes are tiny, deep-fried patties prepared with flour, seasonings, and salted codfish. Their savory taste goes well with bakes, and they have a crispy surface and soft middle.

These are only a few of the mouthwatering and varied regional dishes Barbados has to offer. Bajan cuisine provides a mouthwatering variety of tastes and textures that represent the island's rich cultural background and culinary traditions, ranging from hot stews to sweet sweets.

Wine Tour in Barbados

Barbados has a growing wine industry, while the country is best known for producing rum. The following is a list of some of Barbados' best wineries, along by descriptions of their offerings:

1. Abbey of Saint Nicholas:
- Wines: Saint Nicholas Abbey grows a variety of wines, including rosés, whites, and reds, on its estate. Using traditional winemaking methods, their wines are produced from carefully chosen grapes cultivated on the ancient plantation site.
- Description: Saint Nicholas Abbey's wines are distinguished by their unique terroir, elegance, and complexity. The white wines are crisp and refreshing with notes of citrus and tropical fruits, while the reds are full-bodied with rich fruit flavors and gentle tannins. The rosés have a subtle harmony of fruitiness and acidity, and they are vivid and fragrant.

2. Mount Gay Distillery for Rum:
- Wines: Mount Gay Rum Distillery makes a modest range of wines from grapes produced nearby in addition to their well-known rum. They have three wines: a Cabernet Sauvignon, a Merlot, and a Chardonnay.
- Description: Each variety of Mount Gay's wines reflects the island's tropical environment and limestone-rich soils, showcasing the distinctive terroir of Barbados. The full-bodied, buttery Chardonnay with hints of vanilla and luscious tropical fruits. With notes of spice and

black cherries, the Merlot is silky and mellow. Strong and powerful, the Cabernet Sauvignon has powerful notes of black fruit and a lengthy, lingering aftertaste.

3. The Wine House:
- Wines: Situated in the center of Bridgetown, La Maison du Vin is a boutique winery that specializes in producing artisanal wines in small batches from grapes that are obtained locally. They have a Pinot Noir, a sparkling rosé, and a Sauvignon Blanc among their wines.
- Description: La Maison du Vin produces wines of extraordinary quality and character through painstaking attention to detail throughout the crafting process. The crisp, refreshing Sauvignon Blanc with notes of tropical and citrus fruits. Ripe berry notes and earthy overtones can be found in this beautiful and silky Pinot Noir. With subtle aromas of cream and strawberries, the sparkling rosé is crisp and light.

4. Holder's Residence:
- Wines: A variety of estate-grown wines, including whites, reds, and rosés, are produced at the historic plantation estate known as Holder's House. The grapes used to make their wines are cultivated sustainably in the estate's vineyards.
- Description: The wines produced by Holder's House are renowned for their outstanding quality and unique tastes. With notes of citrus and tropical fruits, the white wines have a lively acidity and are crisp and refreshing. With intricate layers of black fruit and spice, the red wines are velvety and deep. The rosés have a subtle

harmony of fruitiness and acidity, and they are vivid and fragrant.

5. Granny's Winery:
- Wines: Located in the St. Philip parish, Granny's Vineyard is a family-run winery that specializes in organic and biodynamic wines produced from conventional grape varietals. They have a sparkling blanc de blancs, a Chardonnay, and a Cabernet Franc.
- Description: Granny's Vineyard produces clean, expressive, character-filled wines by focusing on sustainability and environmental management throughout the wine-making process. With notes of cedar and cherry, the Cabernet Franc is robust and peppery. With hints of buttered toast and green apple, the Chardonnay is sophisticated and creamy. Crisp and invigorating, the sparkling blanc de blancs has vivid bubbles and a lengthy, lasting aftertaste.

These are just a few of the exceptional wines that Barbados produces. A wine tour in Barbados is sure to be an enjoyable and fulfilling experience, regardless of your level of wine expertise or your desire to just sample the island's gastronomic offerings.

CHAPTER 5: BEAUTY, FITNESS AND HEALTH

Barbados Beauty & Spa

1. Spa at The Crane, Serenity:
- Description: Situated on Barbados' southeast coast, the opulent Crane Resort is home to the Serenity Spa at The

Crane. Massages, facials, body wraps, and beauty services are just a few of the holistic therapies and wellness services provided by this award-winning spa. With views of the ocean and beautiful tropical plants as its backdrop, Serenity Spa offers a restful and revitalizing setting ideal for pampering and relaxation.

2. Sandy Lane Spa:
- Description: Located on Barbados' west coast, the exclusive Sandy Lane Spa is part of the Sandy Lane Resort. A wide range of spa services, such as massages, body treatments, facials, and beauty therapies, are available at this top-notch facility. In an elegant and tranquil environment, guests may enjoy sumptuous treatments influenced by both worldwide wellness approaches and ancient Bajan customs.

3. Coral Reef Club's Spa:
- Description: Located within the classy Coral Reef Club hotel on Barbados' west coast is The Spa at Coral Reef Club. Body scrubs, massages, facials, and beauty therapies are just a few of the holistic treatments and health services provided by this small spa. In the tranquil surrounds of the spa's vast tropical gardens, visitors may unwind and rest while receiving individualized treatments catered to their specific requirements.

4. Limegrove Lifestyle Center: Ayesha's Salon:
- Description: The Salon by Ayesha is situated in Holetown, Barbados, within the exclusive Limegrove

Lifestyle Centre. A variety of hair, nail, and cosmetic treatments are provided by this little salon, such as haircuts, styling, coloring, manicures, pedicures, and waxing. The staff of skilled stylists and beauty therapists at the salon offers individualized treatments in a stylish, contemporary setting.

5. Sapphire Salon for Hair and Nails:
- Description: Situated in the center of Bridgetown, Barbados, Sapphire Hair and Nail Studio is a full-service salon. A comprehensive variety of hair, nail, and beauty treatments are provided by this locally owned and run salon, including haircuts, styling, coloring, manicures, pedicures, and waxing. The experienced and amiable personnel at the salon is dedicated to giving customers excellent treatments in a laid-back setting.

6. Spa & Beauty Lounge Indulgence:
- Description: Situated in the heart of Warrens, Barbados, lies Indulgence Spa and Beauty Lounge. A variety of spa and beauty services, such as massages, facials, body treatments, manicures, pedicures, and waxing, are provided by this contemporary facility. In the peaceful settings of the spa, patrons may rest and relax while indulging in customized treatments intended to improve their appearance and overall health.

7. Barbados's The Westin Resort & Spa's Heavenly Spa by Westin:
- Description: Situated inside The Westin Resort & Spa on Barbados' southern coast is Heavenly Spa by Westin.

Numerous spa services, such as massages, facials, body treatments, and cosmetic therapies, are available at this modern facility. In the tranquil setting of the spa, patrons may revitalize both their bodies and minds by indulging in therapies that promote rest, well-being, and renewal.

These are just a few of Barbados' best spas and beauty parlors. These facilities provide a variety of treatments to suit your requirements, whether you're looking for relaxation, renewal, or a makeover. This guarantees a pampering experience that will leave you feeling renewed and invigorated.

Barbados Fitness and Gym Facilities

1. The Surfside Wellness Center:
- Description: Located on Barbados' southern shore, Surfside Wellness Centre is a top training facility with a variety of exercise courses and cutting-edge equipment. The gym has free weights, strength training equipment, and cardio machines in addition to spaces set out for spinning, group exercise, and personal training. In addition, members get access to facilities including showers, locker rooms, and free towel service.

2. The Crane Resort's Fitness Center:
- Description: Located within the opulent Crane Resort on Barbados' southeast coast, The Fitness Centre at The Crane Resort is a fully furnished gym. The gym has a wide range of functional training spaces, weight training

equipment, and cardio machines. Additionally, guests may take advantage of group exercise programs taught by professional instructors in yoga, Pilates, and Zumba.

3. The Barbados Aquatic Centre's gymnasium:
The Barbados Aquatic Centre's Gymnasium is a state-of-the-art exercise center situated in Wildey, Barbados. The gym has free weights, functional training sections, and a variety of cardio and strength training equipment. A range of fitness courses and programs, such as circuit training, HIIT, and boot camp exercises, are available to members.

4. Fit For Life Fitness Center Open 24/7:
- Description: Situated in the center of Bridgetown, Barbados, Fit For Life 24 Hour Fitness Centre is a 24-hour fitness facility. Fitness aficionados of all skill levels may find what they need at the gym's extensive selection of cardio machines, weight training tools, and functional training spaces. Members get access to the facilities 24/7 and may take use of services including parking, lockers, and showers.

5. Club Fidelity Fitness:
- Description: Offering small group fitness programs and individualized instruction, Fidelity Fitness Club is a boutique gym situated in Rockley, Barbados. The gym offers a range of functional training facilities, outdoor exercise locations, and cardio and strength training equipment. Members may take part in TRX, kettlebell, and circuit training programs as well as work with

licensed personal trainers to reach their fitness objectives.

6. Life Fitness Center:
- Description: Life Fitness Centre is a family-run gym in Hastings, Barbados, that provides exercise lovers of all ages with a welcoming and encouraging atmosphere. Along with a variety of cardio machines, weight training tools, and group exercise sessions, the gym also offers individualized training plans and dietary guidance. In addition, members have access to massage treatment, a steam room, and a sauna.

7. Kurt Gym's body:
- Description: Known for its dynamic group exercise sessions and individualized training plans, Body By Kurt Gym is a well-liked fitness facility in Warrens, Barbados. The gym has a range of exercise equipment, such as functional training zones, strength training machines, and cardio machines. Members have access to expertly instructed sessions in circuit training, kickboxing, and spin.

These are just a few of the best fitness facilities and gyms in Barbados. These facilities provide a range of tools, programs, and services to support you in reaching your wellness and health objectives, regardless of your level of experience or where you are in your fitness journey.

CHAPTER 6: BARBADOS ITINERARY FOR 7 DAYS

Day 1: Arrival and leisurely beach time
Morning:
- Get to Barbados and make sure your lodging is ready.

- Savor a leisurely breakfast at a restaurant or café in the area.
- Visit a well-known Barbados beach, such Crane Beach or Accra Beach, and spend the morning swimming in the blue waves and lounging on the fine sand.

In the afternoon:
- Grab a picnic from the neighborhood store or have lunch at a restaurant along the beach.
- Visit neighboring sites including George Washington House and the Barbados Museum and Historical Society.
See the spectacular views of the Caribbean Sea by stopping at viewing sites during a picturesque drive along the coast.

Evening:
- Savor fresh fish and regional Bajan cuisine for supper at a restaurant on the waterfront.
Savor the breathtaking hues of the setting sun as you take a romantic sunset boat along the shore.
- Take a leisurely walk down the beach under the starry sky to round off the evening.

Day 2: Rum Distillery Tour and Island Exploration

Morning:
- Begin the day with a substantial breakfast in the café nearby or at your lodging.

- Set off on an island trip to see Barbados' scenic landscapes and iconic cultural sites. See places like Animal Flower Cave, Hunte's Gardens, and Harrison's Cave.

In the afternoon:
- Have a picnic in a beautiful location on the island or stop for lunch at a typical Bajan restaurant.
- Go on a guided tour of one of the well-known rum distilleries in Barbados, such Foursquare or Mount Gay. Discover the background and methods of manufacture of the most well-known export from Barbados.

Evening:
- After the day's events, go back to your lodging to unwind and change.
- Enjoy delectable Bajan fare and rum drinks for supper at a nearby restaurant.
- Take in the lively nightlife of Barbados by attending a seaside bar or club where live music and entertainment are provided.

Day 3: Outdoor Activities and Adventure
Morning:
- Before starting a day of outdoor sports and adventure, fuel yourself with breakfast.
- Visit Barbados' east coast to discover rocky beaches and stunning hiking paths. See the magnificent rock formations and roaring surf at Bathsheba Beach.

In the afternoon:

- Eat lunch in a café by the shore, taking in the gorgeous views of the water and the relaxed environment.
- Take part in water sports on the coral reefs, including surfing, paddleboarding, or snorkeling.

Evening:
After a full day of exploration, go back to your lodging to rest and recuperate.
Have a peaceful supper at a nearby eatery while indulging on delicacies from the Caribbean and fresh seafood.
Go stargazing or take a moonlight walk along the beach in the evening.

Day 4: Shopping and Cultural Immersion
Morning:
- Begin your day with a typical Bajan breakfast at a nearby restaurant, where you can try specialties like cou-cou and flying fish.
- Visit historical sites like St. Nicholas Abbey, Bridgetown and its Historic Garrison, and the Nidhe Israel Synagogue and Museum to fully immerse yourself in Barbados' rich cultural legacy.

In the afternoon:
- Stroll around the lively streets of Bridgetown, the capital city of Barbados, and peruse the markets and stores there to find handicrafts and gifts.
- Sample Bajan street food delicacies like fish cakes and fried plantains while having lunch at a quaint café or street food seller.

Evening:
- Go back to your lodging to unwind and change before supper.
Savor a night on the town while sipping drinks at Bridgetown's hip pubs and lounges.
- Finish the evening with a delectable meal at a restaurant that serves Bajan fusion or other foreign cuisine.

Day 5: Rest and Well-Being
Morning:
- Rejuvenate your body and mind by doing yoga or meditation on the beach to connect with nature and start the day.
- Dine at a wellness cafe or restaurant and enjoy a nutritious breakfast that includes smoothies, fresh fruit, and regional delicacies.

In the afternoon:
- Reward yourself with a spa day at one of Barbados' opulent health facilities, such Sandy Lane Spa or Serenity Spa at The Crane. Savor body treatments, facials, and massages that are intended to help you unwind and feel good.

Evening:
- Conclude your journey toward wellbeing with a meditation session on the beach or a yoga class after sunset.

- Enjoy a thoughtfully cooked meal in a health-conscious restaurant using organic and locally sourced foods.
- Indulge in a private jacuzzi or a soothing bath scented with essential oils as you unwind in the luxury of your lodging for the evening.

Day 6: Water Activities and a Beach Day
Morning:
- Start the day with a leisurely breakfast at your lodging or a café on the beach to prepare for a fun-filled day in the sun.
Go to one of the stunning beaches in Barbados, such Bottom Bay or Mullins Beach, and spend the morning swimming, tanning, and making sandcastles.

In the afternoon:
- Enjoy a beachside meal with refreshing seafood and exotic beverages for lunch.
- Take part in aquatic sports like coast-side jet skiing, parasailing, or catamaran sailing.

Evening:
- After a fun-filled day at the beach, get back to your lodging to rest and recover.
Savor a beachside cookout supper while watching the sun set and cooking fresh seafood and meats.
- Attend a beach bar or nightclub in the evening to enjoy live music and dance outside beneath the stars.

Day 7: Leave and Say Goodbye to Barbados
Morning:

Savor your favorite delicacies at your farewell breakfast in Barbados as you take in your last minutes on the island.
- Enjoy a leisurely walk along the shore.

perhaps make one more trip around neighboring sites before leaving your lodging.

In the afternoon:
- Make your way to the airport to board your journey home, saying goodbye to the beautiful island of Barbados.
- Consider the wonderful moments and experiences you had while visiting Barbados.

Evening:
- Take the generosity of the Bajan people and the warmth of the Caribbean sun with you when you go from Barbados and return home.

This program provides travelers with a thorough and varied introduction to Barbados, fusing adventure, leisure, cultural immersion, and wellness pursuits to make their trip one to remember.

CHAPTER 7: BARBADOS WEATHER AND CAMPING

Barbados Climate Pattern

Barbados has a year-round tropical climate with pleasant temperatures, plenty of sunlight, and cooling trade breezes. There are two primary seasons on the island: the rainy season (June to November) and the dry season (December to May). Knowing the weather trends in Barbados may aid travelers in making appropriate travel and activity plans.

December to May (dry season)
- Temperature: Barbados normally experiences temperatures between 75°F and 85°F (24°C and 29°C) throughout the dry season. It's the perfect time of year for outdoor activities and beach activities because of the warm, pleasant weather.
- Rainfall: During the dry season, there is little to no rainfall, except for sporadic, fleeting showers or clouds. Long periods of sunny days with clear sky are to be expected, making them ideal for outdoor activities and seeing the island's attractions.
- Humidity: During the dry season, there is less humidity, making it pleasant for visitors to explore the island without feeling unduly sticky or unpleasant.
- Wind: The northeast trade winds provide a cool breeze that moderates temperatures and controls humidity levels. The perfect conditions for water sports like sailing, windsurfing, and kiteboarding make these winds especially welcome to those who enjoy them.

Rainy Season: June through November
- Temperature: Barbados' rainy season experiences temperatures between 75°F and 85°F (24°C and 29°C), which are comparable to those of the dry season. Even

with sporadic sprinkles of rain, the weather is still warm and comfortable for outdoor activities.

- Rainfall: Barbados has more rainfall throughout the rainy season, mostly in the afternoons and nights. These short, heavy downpours are common. Although Barbados is less vulnerable to direct strikes than other Caribbean resorts, tropical storms and hurricanes may still have an impact on the island during this season.

- Humidity: During the rainy season, especially after rainfall, humidity levels rise. It may be rather hot for visitors, particularly in the early morning and late at night.

- Wind: During the rainy season, trade winds continue to blow, offering respite from the heat and humidity. However, depending on atmospheric conditions and weather systems, winds may differ in direction and strength.

Weather-Related Matters for Visitors

- Packing: Travelers should carry light, breathable clothes that is appropriate for warm weather while heading to Barbados. Sun protection is crucial, particularly during the dry season when UV levels are high. This includes wearing hats, sunglasses, and sunscreen.

- Activities: While the wet season may provide chances for cultural encounters, interior attractions, and spa treatments on rainy days, the dry season is best for outdoor adventures, beach activities, and water sports.

- Travel Planning: Especially during the rainy season, travelers should stay tuned to weather reports and tropical storm updates. It could be necessary to modify travel arrangements in the event of bad weather or severe weather alerts.

- Flexible Itinerary: Travelers may maximize their stay in Barbados and adjust to changing weather conditions by having a flexible itinerary. On cloudy or wet days, indoor attractions, museums, and dining establishments might provide alternatives.

All in all, Barbados' climate provides visitors with a year-round combination of warmth, sunlight, and sporadic downpours. Whether traveling in the dry or rainy season, visitors can anticipate an amazing and delightful time seeing the island's natural beauty, rich culture, and must-see sights.

Barbados Camping

Barbados Camping Advice

1. Pick the Perfect Site: Look for a campground that is easily accessible, safe, and well situated close to attractions, hiking trails, or beaches.

2. Examine the Weather Forecast: The weather in Barbados is erratic, so before you go, check the forecast and be ready for any unexpected changes.

3. Pack Light: If you're trekking to your campground, try not to overpack by bringing just the essential camping supplies and gear.

4. Keep Hydrated: Especially while engaging in outdoor activities, remain hydrated by drinking plenty of water in the warm Caribbean environment.

5. Prevent Sunburn: To avoid sunburn and heat exhaustion, wear a hat, sunglasses, and sunscreen often. You should also look for shade during the warmest parts of the day.

6. Respect the Environment: Pack out all rubbish, be mindful of animals, and abide by local camping laws in order to leave no trace.

7. Plan Your Activities: To get the most out of your camping vacation, research and arrange outdoor activities like hiking, swimming, snorkeling, or stargazing.

8. Be Mosquito Ready: Carry bug repellent and mosquito netting to ward against bites, particularly at night and near water sources.

9. Keep yourself safe by being aware of emergency protocols, keeping a first aid kit nearby, and communicating your camping schedule and anticipated return time to someone.

Camping Equipment
- Tent
- A sleeping bag
Comforter or air mattress
- A portable barbecue or stove for camping
- Pots and pans for cooking
- A flashlight or lantern
- Foldable camping stools or chairs
- Foldable table
- A refrigerator to store food

Clothes and Sneakers:

- Breathable and light clothes
- Swimsuits
- A hat or a cap
- Sunglasses
- Robust hiking sandals or shoes
- Sandals or aquatic footwear
- Poncho or raincoat
- Long sleeves and long pants to defend against insects

Personal Requirements:
- Sunscreen with at least SPF 30
- Repellent for insects
- Items for personal hygiene, such as soap, toothpaste, and toothbrushes.
- Towel
- Dishwashing soap that breaks down naturally
- Sanitizer for hands
- Prescription drugs
- Multipurpose tool or little knife

Accessories for the outdoors:
A daypack or a backpack
- Dry sacks or bags that resist water
- A pair of binoculars
- A smartphone or camera to record memories
- Atlases or manuals
- A portable power bank or charger for phones

Food and Hydration:
- An ample supply of potable water (think about packing a water filter device)

- Hydration reservoirs or reusable water bottles
- Food products that don't spoil easily, such dried fruits, almonds, granola bars, and canned foods
- Recently harvested fruits and veggies
- Condiments, spices, and cooking oil
- Bags of tea or instant coffee
- Single-use cups, plates, and cutlery

Amusement and Coziness:
- E-readers, periodicals, or books
- Taking part in card or trip board games
- Musical instruments, such as the ukulele and guitar
- A portable music speaker
A hammock to unwind in
- A beach umbrella or shade canopy

Security and Emergencies:
- A first aid kit that contains bandages, antiseptic wipes, painkillers, and other supplies.
- An emergency whistle
- Water-resistant lighters or matches
- A fire extinguisher
- A GPS or compasse
- Local emergency numbers and emergency contact details
- Personal flotation equipment for boating or swimming

Whether you want to camp in Barbados in the summer or at any other time of year, you'll be ready to have an amazing time if you follow these camping recommendations and carry the essential equipment and supplies.

CONCLUSION

In closing, as you turn the final pages of this travel guide to Barbados, I hope you feel inspired and invigorated by the vibrant tapestry of experiences this island paradise has to offer. From the sun-kissed shores of its pristine beaches to the lush greenery of its tropical landscapes, Barbados beckons with an irresistible allure, captivating the hearts and imaginations of travelers from around the world.

As you've journeyed through the pages of this guide, you've discovered the rich cultural heritage and warm hospitality that define the essence of Barbadian life. You've explored historic landmarks steeped in centuries of tradition, indulged in the tantalizing flavors of Bajan cuisine, and reveled in the rhythm of calypso beats under the starry Caribbean sky.

But beyond the surface beauty lies a deeper connection, a sense of kinship with the land and its people, forged through shared moments of laughter, exploration, and discovery. Whether you've embarked on adrenaline-fueled adventures, basked in the serenity of secluded coves, or simply savored the joy of being present in the moment, Barbados has left an indelible mark on your soul.

As you bid farewell to this enchanting island, may your memories be filled with the sights, sounds, and sensations that have touched your heart and awakened your spirit. And may your journey through Barbados serve as a reminder that the true essence of travel lies not only in the destinations we visit, but in the moments we share and the connections we forge along the way.

So until we meet again, may the spirit of Barbados accompany you wherever your adventures may take you, guiding you with its warmth and grace, and reminding you that the world is a vast and wondrous tapestry, waiting to be explored one unforgettable chapter at a time. Safe travels, and may your next destination be as magical as the paradise you've discovered in Barbados.

Made in the USA
Columbia, SC
19 October 2024

44705219R00065